To Eileen —
With my continued best to
you and your family

Samuel Hazo
4/15/2003

JUST ONCE

JUST ONCE

New and Previous Poems

Samuel Hazo

Autumn House
Press

PITTSBURGH

"Autumn House" and "Autumn House Press" are registered trademarks owned by Autumn House Press, a non-profit corporation.

Text and cover design: Kathy Boykowycz
Editorial consultant: Eva Maria Simms
Marketing consultant: Michael Wurster

Cover photograph: William Albert Allard

Printed in the U.S.A. by Thomson-Shore

ISBN: 0-9669419-5-0
Library of Congress Control Number: 2002107830

This publication was supported in part by the Pennsylvania Council on the Arts, a state agency funded by the Commonwealth of Pennsylvania, and the National Endowment for the Arts, a federal agency.

Mary Anne

AUTUMN HOUSE POETRY SERIES

Michael Simms, editor

OneOnOne
Jack Myers

Snow White Horses, Selected Poems 1972-1988
Ed Ochester

The Leaving, New and Selected Poems
Sue Ellen Thompson

Dirt
Jo McDougall

Fire in the Orchard
Gary Margolis

Just Once, New and Previous Poems
Samuel Hazo

OTHER WORKS BY SAMUEL HAZO

Poetry
As They Sail
The Holy Surprise of Right Now
Silence Spoken Here
Nightwords
The Color of Reluctance
Thank a Bored Angel
To Paris
Quartered
Once for the Last Bandit
Twelve Poems
Blood Rights
My Sons in God
Listen with the Eye
The Quiet Wars
Discovery

Fiction
Stills
The Wanton Summer Air
The Very Fall of the Sun
Inscripts

Criticism
Smithereened Apart: A Critique of Hart Crane
The Autobiographers of Everybody

Essays
The Pittsburgh That Starts Within You
The Feast of Icarus

The Rest Is Prose
Spying for God

Plays
Feather
Solos
Until I'm Not Here Anymore
Mano a Mano: A Flamenco Drama (The Life of Manolete)

Translations
The Pages of Day and Night (Poems of Adonis)
Lebanon: Twenty Poems for One Love
   (Poems of Nadia Tueni)
Transformations of the Lover (Poems of Adonis)
The Growl of Deeper Waters
   (Essays of Denis de Rougemont)
The Blood of Adonis

Chapbooks
Ballads and Duets
Latching the Fist
Shuffle, Cut and Look

ACKNOWLEDGMENTS

Grateful acknowledgment is made to *American Scholar, Arts and Letters, Dickinson Review, Georgia Review, Jusoor, Hudson Review, Laurel Review, Mid-American Poetry Review, Notre Dame Magazine, Notre Dame Review, Pittsburgh Post-Gazette, Samizdat, September 11, 2001: American Writers Respond, Sewanee Review, Shenandoah, Southern Review, Tar River Poetry, Texas Observer, Vital Speeches* and *Water Stone*, in which some of these poems first appeared. Special acknowledgment is made to the University of Arkansas Press for permission to include a selection of poems from *As They Sail* (1999).

Special thanks to William Albert Allard of the *National Geographic* for permission to use his remarkable photograph on the book jacket.

TABLE OF CONTENTS

III

IV

MONOLOGUE OF THE BODY

When I rub suede, my hands
    speak suede.
                    Without my shoes
    I understand the languages of sand
    and stones and grass.
                      Swimming,
    I return to what I was
    when I began, drifting in tides
    more ancient than the stars.
                      Within
    my skin I summer always
    in the stopped and tropic Fahrenheit
    of Borneo.
             Ice burns like fever
    in the furnace of my mouth.
                    My eyes
    drink everything I see.
                  My ears
    consume entire symphonies.
In a blood-rage I rave the way
    a woman once aroused
    tramples the fences of restraint.
Of all my promised days
    I dedicate one-third to sleep,
    one third to obligation, and the rest
    to what I know because
    I feel.
             I live with wounds
    by day.
                By night I heal.

I

THE MOST

Beneath your shoulderblades
    the sea received the length
    of you but not your weight.
You floated, bobbed and watched
    the clouds.
             They taught you
    what indifference means.
                  Then,
    just then you were the sea's
    as you are love's each time
    you cradle little Anna in the valley
    of your arm, her cheek against
    your shaven cheek like satin.
Her tiny life admits you
    to the all-surrounding and ongoing
    present tense that orders
    recollection back into its grave
    and names the future as the dream
    it is.
        It's like what happens
    when the body springs its locks
    and frees itself in tears
    or eases in the last, involuntary
    loosenings that lovers know.
You felt that free one evening
    on the rock paths of La Fondation
    Maeght with Giacometti, Sert,
    Chagall, Kandinsky, Braque
    and other instant friends.
                 Dead,
    they populated every space you saw

as surely as the scents of lavender
and lawns attuned the air
beneath the cypresses.
                              The moment
cancelled thought by making
thinking or the wish to think
unthinkable and quite unwelcome.
It held you like abandonment itself—-
the taste of all that excellence,
the gift of it, the weightlessness.

STRIP POKER: A PARABLE

There's only you and the dealer.
Already naked, she has nothing
  more to lose.
            You're playing
  by her rules with her deck.
She knows you're watching her
  more closely than the cards.
She stands there like a model,
  letting you distract yourself
  until you're down to socks
  and underwear.
              You tell yourself
  her brows and breasts are less
  than perfect, but the sweet scent
  of her lips and the musk from her hips
  are unignorable.
            You bet
  both socks and lose to a royal
  straight flush.
            Since quitting
  is prohibited, you go for broke
  and see your triple sevens
  fade before her triple jacks.
Without your underwear you feel
  much smaller than you are.
"Relax," she says, "we all
  look truer, nude."
            You say
  you never thought you'd hear
  that said by anyone so beautiful
  and, if she'd excuse the word, exposed.

She says, "You had no way
 of knowing, and, besides, what
 difference does it make?
                    All
 those who play this game
 end bare as they began
 and everybody plays.
                    How long
 you play is in the cards.
Some lose at first, some later
 and some finally, but everybody
 loses."
           Another player waits
 for her to deal.
                    He's wearing
 double-trousers, double-neckties,
 double-everything.
                    She knows
 defenses when she sees them,
 but she deals regardless.
Each card comes snapping
 off her fingers with a click.
After he's down to skin,
 the second player asks,
 "Is this game fixed?"
                    "Not fixed,"
 she says, "but totally predictable.
Nobody beats the house, and I'm
 the house.

        I keep on winning
just to prove to you
that losing everything's not
everything.
        You always end
with what you had in the beginning."

CASANOVA TO GOD

I thought of women basically
    as fruit: delectable when ripe,
    dismissable past prime,
    disposable when old.
                    I'm not
    to blame.
             You made young women
    irresistible, not I.
              My sin—·
    if it was sin at all—was ultimate
    enjoyment of Your handiwork.
That girl from Padua—the supple
    once-ness of her kiss....
                  Her cousin
    from Trieste—the way her breasts
    announced themselves....
                 Surely
    You appreciate the patience and the skill
    it takes to bring a virgin
    to the point where shame means nothing.
I'm not a rapist, after all.
The ones I chose were single,
    willing, totally agreeable.
They wanted to be loved deliciously.
Not roughly like those toughs who pinched
    them on the street, but step
    by gentle step and never in a hurry.
First, some conversation.
               Then,
    a kiss on either cheek.
Then everything that You alone

could see: a jettison of clothes,
my palm along her inner thigh,
our loins in juncture as we hugged,
the mounting puffs and shudders
on the sheets, the parting, the repose.
It made me marvel at the way
You fashioned us for mating
face to face—essentially
two kinds of kissing happening
in one position all at once.
Because I reached perfection in the act,
some called me a philanderer...
Pronounce me guilty if You like...
I'm reconciled.
I did what I
alone could do when I could
do it.
Who says desire dies?
Today I'm tended by a nurse
who spoons me noodles from a cup.
She tells me to relax.
Relax?
When a woman naked underneath
her whites and silks is just a breath
away from Giacomo Girolamo
Casanova of Venice?
Impossible.

INTIFADA

Singly at first, then doubly,
    then slowly by the tens or twenties,
    then steadily on....
                    Interviewed
    about the deathcount in Ramallah,
    one sergeant said, "We'll kill
    them all, but we'll never
    forgive them for making us do it."
Later he aimed his Uzi at a boy
    armed with a stone and a slingshot.
One general claimed his soldiers
    fired only rubber-coated bullets.
When asked about the difference
    to the dead, he frowned and shouted,
    "Their leaders and parents use
    these children as human shields."
Despite the contradicting photographs,
    pundits and lobbyists concurred.
After all, who could deny
    that boys with all their lives
    ahead of them would happily
    seek execution, that mothers loved
    to see their sons in open
    coffins, that choosing a brave
    death instead of a lifelong one
    was an option for fools?
                    No one
    would claim that occupation
    to the occupied resembled daily
    suffocation.

No one would add
that suffocation or the fear of it
begot a courage born
of desperation.
No one compared it
to the fate of being locked
in darkness in a stalled elevator
underground.
Like someone buried
upright and alive, anyone
trapped there would stop at nothing.

THE FIRST SAM HAZO AT THE LAST

A minor brush with medicine
   in eighty years was all
   he'd known.
             But this was different.
His right arm limp and slung,
   his right leg dead to feeling
   and response, he let me spoon him
   chicken-broth.
            Later he said
   without self-pity that he'd like
   to die.
        I bluffed, "The doctors
   think that therapy might help you
   walk again."
          "They're liars,
   all of them," he muttered.
              Bedfast
   was never how he hoped to go.
"In bed you think of everything,"
   he whispered with a shrug, "you think
   of all of your life."
          I knew
   he meant my mother.
           Without her
   he was never what he might have been,
   and everyone who loved him knew it.
Nothing could take her place—
   not the cars he loved to drive,
   not the money he could earn at will,
   not the roads he knew by heart
   from Florida to Saranac, not the two

replacement wives who never
measured up.
                    Fed now by family
or strangers, carried to the john,
shaved and changed by hired help,
this independent man turned silent
at the end.
                Only my wife
could reach him for his private needs.
What no one else could do
        for him, he let her do.
She talked to him and held
        his hand, the left.
                    She helped him
bless himself and prayed beside him
        as my mother might have done.
"Darling" was his final word
        for her.
                Softly, in Arabic.

THE LADY FROM BULGARIA

My son, his son and I
    unseal the first and largest
    lady from Bulgaria.
                        Wooden
    and squat as a Buddha, she comes
    apart exactly at the waist
    and splits into halves the size
    of cups.
                Inside resides
    a second lady from Bulgaria.
Cracked, she's like an erne's
    egg, halved.
                    Inside's
    a third lady from Bulgaria.
She also splits to show
    the final lady from Bulgaria,
    small as a primal seed
    and stern as a sphinx.
                        Hatching
    these ladies from Bulgaria
    is hardly creative.
                    At best
    it's only something to do.
Who conjured up this fantasy
    in wood, and what's the point?
Was it to show that inside
    every woman is another
    woman and another and another?
Which one provoked Montaigne
    to say, "She holds one lover
    in her arms, but another in her thoughts?"

Which one redeemed the Bishop
        of Hippo or schooled Abe Lincoln
        in the wilderness?
                        Which one,
        unclothed or clothed, could make
        the man who wanted her forget
        for once his date with death?
My son remembers who—-
        exactly who—made this
        a gift to us.
                        And when.
                                    And where.
Since puzzles challenge every
        little boy, my grandson sees
        this puzzle as a toy.
                        The puzzle's
        strewn between the three
        of us like shells.
                        What's left
        but to reverse the order and restore
        this litter of ladies from Bulgaria
        in sequence back to one.
                        "All done,"
        my grandson says as if
        we've only played a game—-
        a trio of Sams in a huddle,
            and each with my father's name.

AFTER ARLINGTON

It lasts like a parade in place
    with only the essentials cut
    in rhyming white headstones:
    last names, initials,
    rank, branches of service.
The names answer up in a muster
    of silence while Washington's aglut
    with traffic, vectoring jets
    and disproportion.
                Maple groves,
    roadsigns and gardens
    remember Lady Bird and LBJ.
Facing the Department of Commerce,
    Reagan's billion-dollar
    palace rivals in square
    feet the whole damn Pentagon.
Roosevelt's granite marker,
    scaled as he asked to the length
    and width of his desk, is harder
    to find.
          Jack Kennedy,
    his widow, two children
    and his brother share one plot.
Across the slow Potomac,
    the names in black marble
    of 58,000 futile deaths
    consecrate less than an acre.

BALLAD OF A GRUNT

It's not that we slept in the open.
It's not that we marched in the mud.
It's just that our bosses
made light of our losses
in battles we paid for in blood.

We studied the maps of the country.
We numbered each hill with a name.
But all that we learned
while the villages burned
was how much we were pawns in a game.

When the Cardinal gave us his blessing,
and the movie stars came with their songs,
we laundered our skivvies
and acted like civvies
and then went a-gunning for Congs.

At home there were protests and rallies.
The President said we were brave.
But the generals lied
while the corporals died
in the towns we demolished to save.

This morning we bled in the delta.
Tomorrow we'll bleed in the fields.
In a decade or two
who'll remember the few
who flew back to their graves on their shields?

THE VOICE OF ERNEST HEMINGWAY

Strange that a man who wrote
   alone so trenchantly
   should be averse to microphones.
His Nobel Speech, shorter
   than Faulkner's but as absolute,
   was taped clandestinely by Radio
   Havana.
             Hearing it, you catch
   the same electrical staccato
   that opens *A Farewell to Arms*.
He's generous to fellow penmen,
   skeptical of fame and camaraderie
   and what they do to writers
   who pursue them, candid
   in claiming that the best is what's
   been not yet done but cognizant
   of those who tried courageously
   and failed well trying.
                   But
   it's the voice, his voice—-
   throaty with an almost Spanish
   passion—that can't be unremembered.
For similarity imagine what
   a strong wind does to a high
   flag—the taut fury
   of something staying firmly
   and decisively in place—the poetry
   of utter and intelligent defiance—
   the sinew in the sound—the certainty.

HEMINGWAY PAST, HEMINGWAY PRESENT

"A courageous fool" was how
    Jim Harrison described him.
                                True,
to a point....
                     Aristotle would have called
    bravado much of Hemingway's
    "grace under pressure," but where's
    the poetry in that?
                   War,
    boxing, hunting and bullfights
    were only subjects to be
    re-imagined into words that made
    the re-imagining convincing.
                        That
he could do and did.
                    As for
    his need to court real danger
    just to feel alive, that was
    courageously foolish—agreed.
Or was it?
               If courage braces us
    to do what's right repeatedly,
    then courage for thrills is foolish.
But if it's blind as faith,
    then foolishness condemns the agent,
    not the act.
               The act endures
    thereafter on its own.
                   Aside
    from these distinctions, why
    should talent answer to philosophy

or anything except what dares it
always to be true?
                         "A man's
being a murderer is nothing against
his prose," wrote Oscar Wilde.
Excluding madness or bewitchery,
        Wilde was right.
                         Conversely,
sanctity and artistry with words
are not, with certain exceptions,
synonymous.
                         Either way the only
truth that lasts is on the page.
Everything else is gossip.

WHEN NOTHING'S HAPPENING,
EVERYTHING'S HAPPENING

There's something "old school"
    about you, Charles, and that's
    what I admire most.
                    You still
    believe in friendship, manners,
    duty, generosity and Launceston.
I've never been to Launceston.
Your postcards proffer me a proper
    Norman town in Cornwall
    topped by a castle.
                I'm told
    that all your townsmen know
    who Mr. Causley is, and why not?
You schooled three generations there
    for half a century.
             That keeps
    you dearer to your kin than all
    your books.
          But it was books
    that paired us for a shared recital
    under Shakespeare's shadow.
                  After
    Stratford, it was letters, phone
    calls, meeting once in Washington
    and once in Pittsburgh.
             Now
    it's messages through mutual friends.
Or poetry—especially your dream
    about your parents on a picnic.

Dead for decades, they're sharing tea
        and stoppering a milk-jug
        with a "screw of paper."
                            They wave
        for you to join them in a feast
        that's a reprise of Eden.
                            They're young
        and happy and in love, and the Cornish
        sky shines brighter than the borealis
        through your last (and lasting) words....
Your letters last as well, and that
         includes the jotted postscripts
        on the outside flaps.
                            It's so damn
        good to read what keeps alive
        what's dearest to a man.
                            It shows
        we're not enslaved to memory
        or mere presumption—born liars
        both.
                    It says the present perfect
        is the only tense in any tongue,
        which means the past is now
        whenever poets breathe it
        into life again.
                    So here's
        to the poet from Launceston.
                            And here's
        to his paper and ink.

And here's
to the poems born of his pen
that help us to feel what we think.
So, long live the books that he's written
and long live the books that he'll write
like bread for the dead in the morning
and eyes for the blind at night.

BALLAD OF THE ONE-LEGGED MARINE

My left leg was gone with the boot still on—
the boot that I laced in the morning.
I felt like a boy who had stepped on a toy
and made it explode without warning.

They choppered me back to a medical shack
with no one but corpsmen to heed me.
I stared at the sky and prayed I would die,
and I cursed when the nurse came to feed me.

I knew that I must, so I tried to adjust
while orderlies struggled to teach me
the will of the crutch and the skill of the cane
and assured me their methods would reach me.

The President came with his generals tame
and explained why he never relieved us.
But the red, white and blue of my lone, right shoe
told the world how he lied and deceived us.

They buried my shin and my bones and my skin
an ocean away from this writing.
But pain finds a way on each given day
to take me straight back to the fighting

when I served with the Corps in a slaughterhouse war
where we tallied our killings like cattle,
as if these explain why the armies of Cain
behave as they do in a battle...

Whatever's a bore, you can learn to ignore,
but a leg's not a limb you like leaving.
So you deal with regret and attempt to forget
what always is there for the grieving.

If you look for a clue while I stand in a queue,
you can't tell what's real from prosthetic.
I walk with a dip that begins at my hip,
but I keep it discreet and aesthetic.

If you're ordered on line and step on a mine,
you learn what it means to be only
a name on a chart with a hook in your heart
and a life that turns suddenly lonely.

Lose arms, and you're left incomplete and bereft.
Lose legs, and you're fit for a litter.
Lose one at the knee, and you're just like me
with night after night to be bitter.

For Ray Fagan

SCIENTIA NON EST VIRTUS

"The good that I would I do not;
the evil that I would not, that I do."
                                    St. Paul

After a week in Paris he saw
        in a sign a word he'd never
        learned.
                        Stopping a passerby,
        he asked in French if he
        were French.
                        The response in French
        could best be rendered as "perhaps..."
A month would pass before
        his laundress asked if many
        in America wrote poetry.
He told her there were thousands.
"But," she insisted, "do you have
        one Baudelaire?"
                        Such anecdotes
        not only give new meaning
        to nuance but demonstrate
        how ignorance differs from knowledge,
        and knowledge from holy wisdom.
Though ignorance at best means nothing,
        knowledge may stay the fool of villainy,
        while villainy plays weevil to the will.
And what's the will except a wayward
        stallion ridden by our dreams
        to glory or perdition?
                        For every
        Shakespeare, Lincoln or St. Matthew

there's a murderer, liar, reprobate
or whore who mastered the Brittanica
but stayed the same.
                        Old or young,
we learn too late that being
good is more than strict adherence
to commandments, laws or codes,
much more than being well
informed, and lightyears more
than all the learning in the world.
What is morality but shunning
    deeds we just can't do even
    when the opportunities present
    themselves?
                        It's reflex
    more than choice or reasoning....
If that sounds like a substitute
    for ignorance, then ignorance it is.
If it seems paradoxical
    but vaguely possible, it's knowledge.
If it makes sense, it's wisdom.

WHILE WALKING ON FRANCE

Call it the time of bread
    in Cannes: baguettes in stacks
    like ammunition, jumbled croissants
    and bins of buns and rolls.
At the hotel desk, Sonya
    and Nadeige sing the French
    they speak.
                Madame Antoine,
    whose son Deleuse, Cannonier
    1st Class, died at twenty
    in Algeria, carefully counts coins.
Postcards on the Rue d'Antibes
    remember Gary Cooper, Grace Kelly,
    Bardot, Gabin and Robert Mitchum.
At the Moulin de Mougins a festival
    ago, Sharon Stone bankrolled
    a banquet for AIDS.
                Villas
    in "high" Cannes nestle (yes,
    like nests) in grottoes guarded
    by monitors and bougainvillea.
                Bentleys,
    Daimlers and Porsches cruise
    the Autoroute as privately
    as hearses for the totally enclosed.
Sepulchrally asprawl on beaches
    loll the supine and the prone,
    their tans proceeding by degrees.
Beside a hotel pool a girl
    strips to one triangular string
    to model swimsuits for the trade....

This land where taste is king
    and genuine panache is queen
    attracts and puzzles me.
Does French reluctance spring
    from stubbornness or thought?
What prompts French chocolatiers to make
    the package more seductive than the purchase?
Who but these slim-skulled brothers
    of Rimbaud accord great chefs
    a reverence reserved for kings
    or popes?
                Each time that France
    is underfoot I memorize
    but never judge why pigeons
    chortle the only song
    they know, how palms upsurge
    into a fountainhead of leaves,
    or why the twin born last
    in France is legally the elder...
As men essentialize and women
    existentialize, I focus on ideas
    but ignore the facts.
                The facts,
    I come to see, are France.
                They state
    their own philosophy.
                The more
    I know of it, the less
    I understand.
                The less I understand,
    the more I know that some
    confusions never yield to reason.

UNDERSTORY

It's not that sometimes I forget.
I'm told that everybody does.
What troubles me is how
    whatever I've forgotten trebles
    in importance the more I keep
    forgetting it.
                Some word....
                      Some place....
Today a student from the Class
    of Way Back When
    seemed certain I'd remember him
    by name.
              I tried and tried
    before I had to ask....
                  Though students
    and ex-students are my life,
    I must admit that I remember
    most of the best, all
    of the worst, many who have left
    this world and not that many
    of the rest.
              It leaves me wondering....
Is memory a beast that sheds
    its baggage as it goes?
Are facts by definition destined
    for oblivion?
             Or is it absolute
    that what I can't forget no matter
    how I try is all that's worth
    remembering?
             I know a mother

of four sons who mixes up
their names.
                        Ollie is Bennett.
Bennett is Drew.
                        Drew
is Christopher.
                        Facing one,
she'll travel down the list before
she'll ask, "Tell me your name,
dear boy."
                        Outsiders realize
they're all one boy to her,
regardless of their names.
                        She knows
them by their souls.
                        That reassures me.

For JoAnn Bevilacqua-Weiss

INNOCENT BYSTANDERS ARE NEITHER
INNOCENT NOR BYSTANDERS

Question: What is the most dangerous
profession in the world
today?
Answer: Innocent bystander.

It's easy to talk when the creek's
    a trickle or just a meandering
    fuse of slime between dry rocks.
But what will you say when the creek's
    a stream, and the stream's in flood,
    and the flood's upon you?
                        What
    will you do?
                Angry brown
    water's as deaf as falling
    bombs or charging bulls.
If you are spared, you'll wonder
    why you happened to be standing
    in the way.
             Why you?
                  Why there?
But then why not?
            Later
    you'll do what most survivors do—-
    live recklessly, live all
    you can, live till it hurts.
In time the hurt will be enough
    to make you think.
                You'll cultivate
    an interest in biography.

                              You'll read
        about those kings who, facing death,
        insisted that their tea be brewed
        henceforth from women's tears.
You'll learn how frail Sir Antony
        dined morning, night and noon
        on lobster tails until the last.
You'll be intrigued but unimpressed.
To feel much less alone
        you'll travel to decountrify yourself,
        confide in sympathetic strangers
        and return to what's no longer
        quite the same as home.
                              You'll turn
        from one diversion to another,
        and they'll never seem to end.
But somehow they will help you
        in the way a mirror curved
        behind a bar convinces solitary
        drinkers that they have at least
        and still and finally one friend.

THE FACE OF EVIL IN OUR TIME

"...the banality of evil..."
                        Hannah Arendt

"The Devil's cleverest wile is to convince
us that he does not exist."
                        Charles Baudelaire

Passport-photo plain: Dillinger
        in golfer's slacks, Landru
        relaxing like the altar boy
        he was, Stalin of the "Uncle Joe"
        mustache with Edgeworth pipe-
        tobacco glowing in his calabash,
        Hitler summering in Berchtesgaden.
No fangs, no madman's drool,
        scarcely a sneer.
                        They look
        as common as the rest of us.
Yet Dillinger killed men for sport.
Landru, who poisoned and reduced
        to ash more women than the court
        could number, doodled his trial
        away and smiled in the guillotiner's
        face.
                Killing his country's
        match of Sweden's total
        census was Stalin's way
        of keeping Russia Leninized.
And Hitler's legacy needs only
        to be known to horrify again.
Of the aforementioned who looks

the least suspicious or the most
innocuous?
Possibly all four....
Who said that crimes and criminals
must rhyme?
Manson and his kind
have poisoned us with melodramatized
debauch, satanic symbols,
blood on the ceiling.
Whether
they kill just once or seriatim,
we like our murderers depraved.
As usual, we're wrong.
Real evil
at its worst does not declare
itself.
It cowers like the smallest
of the smallest cancers on a slide,
happy if it's never seen
or else mistakenly identified.
Basic humanity and the inability
to live with guilt prevent
the basest criminals from saying
what they are.
So jails are filled
with innocent men who plead
the sweet hypocrisy of looking
nondescript or temporarily insane.
Likewise, the lawful hell called war
seems absolutely interchangeable
with murder in cold blood.

My-Lai, where villagers
    were "wasted but not killed,"
    made murder murderless.
                    And what
    of all those Filipino nurses
    in Chicago strangled one
    by one five decades back?
The strangler was a handyman named
    Speck.
            Condemned without parole,
    he fattened unremorsefully in prison
    and enjoyed his sentence.
                    Speck
    was his Christian name....
                    Speck.

WHEN LIFE TURNS STILL

For years I never understood
    why painters painted so complete
    a contradiction.
                If down and up
    were opposites by definition,
    then stillness and life could not
    be more at odds.
             But how
    explain away Cézanne
    who posed in absolute perfection
    all those apples, grapes, carafes
    and cheeses on a tray—one blink
    of ripeness just before the rot?
Was every still life for Cézanne
    like music to Stravinsky—not horizontal
    melody but vertical sounds
    in sequence heard in separation,
    each one a song unto itself
    like ranks in a parade?
             Stravinsky's
    theory was to make us listen up
    instead of listen on.
             And that
    made sense.
             If life could end
    at any moment, every moment
    was eternal and unique.
               Ergo,
    Cézanne.
        Ergo, Stravinsky.

Stillness and verticality versus
        motion and protraction....
Last night I saw a woman
        in her sixties whom I dated
        when she turned nineteen.
                                I still
        remember how she curled against
        my shoulder when we danced—-
        the scent of lily in her hair,
        the oval of her waist.
                        Seeing
        how time had made a raisin
        of her face, I understood the sacred
        once of everything and how
        the truthful lies of art
        seem truer than our passing lives.
Is it so wrong to show impossibility
        the factual defiance of a dream?
To say what was still is
        because it was?
                        To lead us
        grudgingly through silence
        into gratitude?
                        Let us
        keep still.
                        Let us be grateful.

LIFE PAINTING

Three days of laundry wait
   for her at home.
                Her neck
   is stiff from posing.
                 Twice
   minimum wage is what she's earning,
   and the class is mixed.
                Her nipples
   harden in the cold.
               She itches
   where she'd never scratch herself
   in public.
           She tries to think
   about the wash and how abundantly
   the sheets will billow in the dryer....
Females behind their easels
   see her merely as another
   of their kind, observing where
   she's fat and where she's not.
They sketch her face with more
   attention than they give the rest
   of her.
          The men see more—-
   a woman nakedly employed—-
   twin dimples in her lower
   back—the vortex in the loins
   where all desires end,
   and life's set free.
             Desire's
   in the air.

The men pay less
attention to the woman's face
than to her thighs.
Someone
announces that the sitting's over.
The painters pack their tubes
and brushes.
Seen from above
the class might seem a tight
isosceles of billiard balls
transformed from nouns to verbs
precisely when the cue ball
strikes.
They scatter to their lives.
The model reaches for her robe.
She scans each drying canvas
as she leaves.
Not one resembles her.

LITTLE (GOD'S) CREATURE

"Do you want to know what love is? Get a dog."
                                    Mona Van Duyn

Simply by lying down and being
        dog, he demonstrates how
        satisfaction differs from fulfillment.
Oscar's fulfilled.
                        Without
        a clock he knows the time
        of night, of year, of age.
So far his only fears are horses,
        storms and any fellow dog
        too large or amorous for comfort.
A miniature horse, he prances
        to his meals, eschewing dogchow
        totally unless disguised.
In cars he rides shotgun—
        head periscoping out the window,
        ears sleeked and flattened
        by the wind, eyes orientaled
        into squints and taking aim.
What makes me love this pooch
        who weighs no more than both
        my shoes?
                        Is it his absolute
        defiance when he fights?
                                Is it
        because he pays attention
        and accepts contentment as life's
        best reward?
                        Is it because

he thinks precisely with his nose
and chats concisely with his tail?
Or is it just his irreplaceability?
Each night he lies beside me
    while I read.
                In dog's arithmetic
    he's half my age, but catching up....
How innocent he is of malice,
    treachery, impatience, envy
    and the fear of death.
                    I read.
He sleeps.
        We share mortality
    in silence, breath by breath.

II

THE FOURTEEN HAPPY DAYS OF
ABD AL-RAHMAN III

"I have known only fourteen happy days in my life."
                    Last words of Abd Al-Rahman III

The first was when he heard
   her name: Azahara.
               The second
was the time he met her
and decided that the caliphate
would be an empty throne
without her.
               The third was when
he married her.
               The fourth
was how she came to him
without her veils.
               He touched
her nipples like the very grapes
of God, loosened her hair
and later felt her inner
thighs against his flanks
like the soft, strong wings
 of a swan.
               The fifth was the son
she gave him.
               The sixth
he never revealed.
               The seventh
was the year he liberated Andalús
and Córdoba.

The eighth was when
the palace in Medina was completed
as his gift to her.
The ninth
was how she smiled when he named
the glories of the palace: 4,000
columns, 13,700 servants
plus 3,500 pages, eunuchs
and slaves to crumble 1,000 loaves
a day for the palace fish.
The tenth was when he chose
to rule in rags and smear
himself with sand to conquer
vanity.
The eleventh he never
revealed.
The twelfth was when
she died, holding his each
hand and speaking as her final
word his name.
The thirteenth
he never revealed.
The fourteenth
was the day he welcomed death
because it meant he'd never
have to bear the agony
of one more day without her.

THE ORIGINS OF WESTERN LOVE

The Arabs of Andalús bequeathed
   the troubadours a minstrelsy
   where love and passion sang.
Latins ignored the song.
Gaius Valerius Catullus
   and his tribe preferred coupling
   on impulse and praising it in couplets
afterward.
              The mix created
courtly love.
              From courtly love
came all the legends of romance,
and from romance the dream where love
of passion seemed more impassioned
than the passion of love.
              Still, we must
be fair.
            Though wiving and wenching
gave way to wiving or wenching,
a few still lived the passionate
friendship that is marriage.
              But
most remained as permanently
parallel as railroad tracks
that never meet except
at the horizon.
            And even there
it's an illusion.
            No wonder
choosing one another every
day became a chore while coupling

on the sly assumed the guise
of ecstasy.
     But why be righteous?
We're lovers all, and love
  without responsibility is every lover's
  dream of happiness.
        Yet all
  that lasts is not what prompts
  but what survives the act.
        If man's
  a wallet waiting to be spent,
  the question's never whether
  but with whom.
     And why.

        If woman
  is a purse whose body's mouths
  are drawstrung shut until
  she gives herself away,
  the question's never whether
  but with whom.
     And why.
       The Arabs
  thought the why unsayable and sang
  the beauties of the where and when.
Catullus settled for the how.
Both felt they sang the answer then
  to something unexplainable
  before.
    Or since.
      Or now.

A TOAST FOR THE LIKES OF TWO

Who was it wrote, "If women
    had mustaches, they would somehow
    make them beautiful.
                          Look
what they've done with breasts!"
Who disagrees?
                  Doesn't the Bible
    say a woman just an inch
    from death will keep an eye
    for color?
             And don't philosophers
    agree that women sacrifice
    the ultimate on beauty's altar?
And love's....
             Why scoff at that?
Are the male gods of money,
    fame and power more deserving?
What's money but guilt?
                What's fame
    but knowing people you will never
    know will know your name?
What's power but pride translated
    into force?
            Are these worth more
    than what sustains us to the end?
Consider Bertha.
          Eighty, blind
    and diabetic, she believed that death's
    real name was Harold.
             "I want
    to know what Harold has to offer,"
    she would say.

She'd seen
her children's children's children
and presumed she had a poet's right
to give a name to death, if so
she chose.
            Chuckling to herself,
she rocked and waited for this last
adventure in her life....
                        Then
there was Jane, who mothered seven
and left unfinished all her art
by choice as if to prove
that incompleteness is the rule
of life where nothing ends
the way it should...or when.
Two weeks before her funeral
she called all seven to her bed
to say, "I hope to see you all
again...but not right away..."
So here's to the honor of Bertha
and here's to the glory of Jane!
Let them be spoken of wherever
beauty's lovers gather to applaud
the beauty of love.
                    Let them
not rest in peace but thrive
in everlasting action, doing
what they love the most.
                    Who wants
a heaven that's equivalent to one
long sleep?

Those crypted, supine
saints in their basilicas can keep
the dream of their Jerusalem.
                              The soul
was meant for more than that.
Pray for us, St. Bertha
Pray for us, St. Jane.

THE LAST SHALL BE FIRST AND ONLY

If anybody speaks their names,
    I still recall them as they were—-
approachable, intelligent, attractive
and single.
             Shirley, dead
at fifty; Janet, who married
badly; Yvonne, grandmotherly
in Georgia; Rose Anita,
whereabouts unknown, and Susie,
whereabouts unknowable....
                         Each pairing
    at the time seemed right until—-
Today like photos in a yearbook
    they present as real the dream
    I call the past.
                What
does it prove?
                 Looking for love
in the wrong season, never
finding it, then not looking
and being found by it....
Despite a million variations
    that's the formula.
                The rest
is choice and work and mystery
and luck, much luck.
                  Power's
a poor replacement.
                 Money's
poorer, and casual philandering's
the poorest of them all.
                 My wife's
my understander.

In matters of romance
she outranks me in wisdom
as a queen outranks a rook.
Like Siamese twins we're fused
at head, hip and heart.
I hurt
when she hurts, hate anyone
who disconcerts her, mope
if I miss, as I have, a birthday,
and, in short, seem out of sorts
when she's away for long.
We wonder who will die the first.
"If I should linger, promise
me a view where I can see
the flowers."
"Since words are where
I live, just keep the coffin
closed and stand my books on top."
No matter where we are, we stay
in touch by telephone or mail
to say what keeps two souls,
together but alone, alone
together.
On trivia we disagree
but still defend good Democrats,
eat mussels from the selfsame dish,
are bored by monologues from chatterers
and trust a carpenter named Christ
to figure out our praying....
That's not
quite all, but so far that's enough.

BALLAD OF THE OLD LOVERS

"Your body's slowed down, my dearest dear.
Your body's slowed down, my dearest."
"I'm aging, my dear—just aging, I fear.
Each day I keep growing older....
The birds in the trees may never freeze,
but the blood as you age grows colder."

"Remember the days when we used to play
and hug on the sheets of the bed there?
You'd touch me here and touch me here,
and then we would wrestle together?
Instead we lie now like the dead there
and listen all night to the weather."

"Remember the money we managed to save
and planned to enjoy in our sixties?
Well, sixty has come, and sixty has gone,
and what have our savings returned us
but travel in season without a good reason
and tropical sunlight that burned us?"

"Remember the friends we knew, we knew,
when we and our friends were younger?
Where have they gone, and why don't they write,
and why have the decades divided
all those not alive from those who survive
no matter how well they're provided?"

"But why blame our fears on the innocent years?
They're gone and beyond re-living....
Since death's quite efficient, and time's insufficient,
is it asking too much to forgive us

for wanting to stay till the end of the day
and love what the years can still give us?"

"So give me a kiss, my dearest of dears,
and sleep by my side forever.
Let the years come, and let the years go.
We treasure what nothing can sever.
In touch or apart is the same to the heart.
Until death parts us not, we're together."

A TIME OF NO SHADOWS

Immortality?
> Too general a concept.
Some say it's never-ending time,
> which means it's long on myth
> but short on meaning.
> > Some say
> it's never to be known until
> it's ours.
> > Some say, some say....
I stand with those who think
> it could be quick as any instant
> going on and on and on
> within itself like poetry or music
> or a kiss.
> > That comes as close
> as anything to God's "I AM
> WHO AM."
> > No past.
> > > No memory.
No future but the time at hand
> that's passing even as it's born... .
Once I was driving due southeast
> through Pennsylvania.
> > > Highways
> were broad and dangerous and everyone's.
As I ran out of Pennsylvania,
> farm by farm, I noticed
> border signs that welcomed me
> to Maryland where Rand McNally
> said that Maryland began.
I knew the earth was still
> the earth in Maryland or Pennsylvania.

I knew I stayed the same,
    border or no border....
                    From here
into hereafter could be just
like that—our selfsame selves
translated instantly from state
to state to God alone
knows what....
                That's immortality.

WHERE WERE YOU WHEN?

Training for trouble is a waste
   of time.
         It makes you think
   of generals preparing armies
   daily for the last war.
When sellers of insurance
   calculate a policy that covers you
   against explosions, loss
   of fingers, flooding, sleeping
   sickness, lightning, rattlesnakes
   or ricochets, you say you're only
   hoping for a good death,
   regardless of the cause.
            They tell you
   no insurance can assure you that....
Troubles ago, you ran uphill
   and walked downhill.
           Today
   you realize that you were strengthening
   yourself against the unevadable....
You do it still, but now
   your hills are poems you attempt
   to finish, rumors of war
   or policies hatched by fools.
Like anyone confronted by the once
   of anything, you try your best
   to be significant.
          If nothing works,
   at least you tried.
         When critics
   stone you with their looks

or words, you know that most
attempters fared no better....
Why waste your prowess on defence?
Salvation's not a matter
of deterrence by the wise and well
prepared.
It's how you think
and what you do when something
unavoidable confronts you all
at once.
It's always a surprise.

AHEAD OF TIME

Her letter, mailed from Saranac,
 is dated 1926.
     My mother's
writing to my aunt.
      It's two
years since she told her father,
"Dad, I'm marrying Sam
and not the man you had
in mind."
    That's decades more
 than half a century ago.
My mother and my aunt are dead.
I'm well past sixty when I share
 my mother's letter with my wife.
It stills us like a resurrection.
Later I read it to my son
 and to his wife.
     They tell me
 how alive it seems as if
 a woman neither ever knew
 is speaking in this very room
 to each of us.
     The letter's full
 of questions I can answer,
  but the time for answering is over.
I realize my life's already longer
 than my mother's was by almost
 thirty years.
     The letter in my hand
 is older than the two of us.

The more I read, the less
    there is to read until
    I reach the bottom of the page.
The last sentence ends
    with a hyphen.
                    There's no page two.

WORDHOARD

It's not to be skimmed but consulted.
Updated as needed, it offers
   the good, the bad and the neutral
   commingled.
            Like playing cards
   shuffled and tamed into a deck,
   the sheer jumble of this world
   seems much less daunting
   in alphabetical order.
            Each word's
   traced back to its father and mother.
Each name precedes parenthesized
   and hyphenated numbers called
   a lifetime.
            Hitler is no less
   emphasized than Offenbach,
   and Offenbach no more than Paul
   Gauguin or Sophocles.
            Nothing
   or no one of note is excluded
   or censored.
            Tupping as noun
   and tupping as verb mean the same.
Kyriakos Theotokopoulos is simply
   El Greco.
            Subtleties reveal
   their secrets.
            The plural of syllabus?
Syllabuses.
       Of octopus?
            Octopus.

Bound in the graveyard of a living
   book, each word's a feast
   for anyone's feeding.
                         Call it
   the work of the worst of all beasts
   at his best.
                 It's there for the reading.

PERSIFLAGE

It's everywhere.
               Orators
declaim such fluff precisely
and *con brio*, but fluff it stays.
Word-piddlers peddle it, page
    after page.
             Casual words
for a casual age, you say?
I'm not convinced.
              No age
is ever what we think it is.
The round earth stayed round
    when everybody called it flat.
It took a second world war
    to make us fix a number to the first.
I could go on, but why?
In or between wars, what matters
    more than heeding the time
    of our lives in the life of our times?
Real writers say so in their books.
When they're safely dead, we dub
    them prophets who deserve the late
    applause of our attention.
              Meanwhile,
marketeers keep saying money
makes money, and that's sufficient.
Managers claim that time is money,
    and that's efficient.
            Majorities
think it's just change to exchange,
and that's omniscient but branded
deficient by all the above.

What's left?

        Proceeding, I suppose,
on our chosen roads while the light
still holds....

          Real writers have left us
their maps if we need them.

              They all
write the same but with different words.
They wait for the lonely to heed them.
It's never too early to read them.

INVITATION TO THE DANCE

All you who have no role
　　but to be droll and wait to be
　　offended—you dodderers
　　who play at being brave
　　with young men's lives—and you
　　who claim that everybody has
　　a price—, enter this camp
　　of concentration at its best where
　　music makes free.
　　　　　　　　　　　Just sounds,
　　you say?
　　　　　　　Mere sounds?
　　　　　　　　　　　Listen.
No one who listens can hate
　　and hear at the same time.
It contradicts the laws of feeling
　　like talking while kissing.
　　　　　　　　　　　Listen.
Already you are more than who
　　you were, and where you are
　　right now is turning into elsewhere.
Welcome to Alicante, autumn
　　in Tuscany, London in the time
　　of Henry Plantagenet.
　　　　　　　　　　The battle-
　　noise of Agincourt did perish
　　with the battle, but the courtly melodies
　　of France still sing.
　　　　　　　　Listen
　　as you'd listen to the final breath

of one you love—that sacredly,
that quietly.
                    For just that long
you'll learn that songs might fade
but will not fail—if you remember
them or not.
                    No hurt
intended, nobody tortured
or shot, no one for sale....

For SRH

BALLAD OF THE JOLLY BROKER

Nothing was surer amid all the furor
than watching a stock that I picked on a hunch
make rich men of paupers, and paupers of fools,
and all in the pinch that it took to eat lunch.

My betting and cheering took real engineering.
I guessed and I gauged and I bet and I prayed
from the dawn of the bull to the dusk of the bear
where fortunes were waiting and fortunes were made.

The world of percents is a world that resents
whenever its buyouts are less than a steal.
Its language is numbers, and numbers are lethal,
and all that makes sense is the luck of the deal.

You have to like poker to be a good broker.
You have to take chances and hope for the best.
Buy cheap and sell dear is the law of the market,
and woe unto those who forget or protest.

Like any good broker I loved to play poker,
but poker's a gamble where all that you've got
is the lure of the cards and the stack of the chips
and the dice of the draw and the pay of the pot....

I took all my winnings that some called my sinnings
and lived like a king where the snow never fell.
I drank all my juices and swallowed my pills
and bet on the races, and down came hell....

It cost me my wife in the prime of my life.
It made me content with much less than the best.
I worked for the day when I never would work,
and the money was sure, and the honey was rest.

If you'd rather be healthy than feeble and wealthy....
If you'd rather be happy than wed to a bed,
then think of a man with a millionaire's tan
who died half a lifetime before he was dead.

STYMIED

Thirty feet of garden hose coil up
    and hibernate.
                My rake, hoe,
    spade and pick stay where
    I stacked them.
              Idle but ready,
    they keep the relaxed look
    of effort in waiting.
              They say
    all tools ask questions that have just
    one answer.
             Deeper questions
    have many—or none at all.
These keep me frowning when I rake,
    hoe, dig or spray azaleas
    in July.
             The answers never come.
I tell myself some things are not
    to be explained: what keeps us
    standing when we stand, how Groucho
    and T. S. Eliot became good friends,
    why death can never kill
    the dead.
             At last I just resign
    myself.
           So much of life
    still baffles me.
             No tools for that....

FORWARD

This summer we stayed at home,
      but France was no less France
      without us.
                  Spared the penance
of planning, we learned what trees
learn by adding ring
to inner ring while going
nowhere.
            Elsewhere, coaches
were planning for the next season,
politicians for the next campaign,
and manufacturers for next year's
cars.
      No one looked back
or sideways or within or anywhere
but straight ahead and then some....
So what if Abel woke to find
      he'd never speak again,
      or Baker shrank another inch,
      or Charlie struggled to remember
      who he was.
                  For them the "next
      level" was straight down or simply
      where they found themselves....
Remember the day we passed
      the house we called our wedding
      house?
                  Strangers were living there.
The newlyweds we were have aged
      into grandparents now.

We feel
the push of generations, and we can't
push back.
        We see we're different,
but we know we're still the same.
Or so we say....
        Tomorrow's
yesterday by just another name.

SEPTEMBER 11, 2001

1

The hawk seems almost napping
    in his glide.
               His arcs are perfect
    as geometry.
               His eyes hunger
    for something about to panic,
    something small and unaware.
Higher by two thousand feet
    an airbus vectors for its port,
    its winglights aiming dead
    ahead like eyesight.
               The natural
    and scheduled worlds keep happening
    according to their rules....
               "We interrupt
this program...."
               Inch by inch
    the interruption overrules both worlds,
    engulfing us like dustfall
    from a building in collapse.
               The day
    turns dark as an eclipse.
               We head
    for home as if to be assured
    that home is where we left it.

2

Before both towers drowned
    in their own dust, someone
    downfloated from the hundredth floor.
Then there were others—plunging,
    stepping off or diving in tandem,
    hand in hand, as if the sea
    or nets awaited them.
                          "My God,
    people are jumping!"
                          Of all
    the thousands there, we saw
    those few, just those, freefalling
    through the sky like flotsam from a blaze....
Nightmares of impact crushed us.
We slept like the doomed or drowned,
    then woke to oratory, vigils,
    valor, journalists declaring war
    and, snapping from aerials or poles,
    the furious clamor of flags.

III

BALLAD OF A RETURNEE

He knew he was older and taller.
He saw that the towns were the same.
What made them seem suddenly smaller?
What made him feel somehow to blame

for all that was done to a village
to save a surrounded platoon?
The huts were just booty to pillage
on a hillscape as spare as the moon.

A man with one leg saw him walking
and offered him tea on a mat.
They spent the whole afternoon talking
while his wife cooked the head of a cat.

It wasn't his squad he remembered.
It wasn't the sergeant at Hue
who found his lieutenant dismembered
and buried him there where he lay.

What troubled him most were the places
that once were just places to fight.
He thought of the nightfighters' faces
all blackened to blend with the night.

The whores in their teens were forgotten
and so were their overnight dates,
and grown were the idly begotten
whose fathers were back in the States.

He never regretted returning.
At least he had lessened his dread.
But the toll that it took for the learning
was 58,000 dead.

He walked in a daze near the water.
He sat all alone on the shore
like a man making peace with the slaughter,
though the price for this peace was war.

DINING WITH MONTAIGNE

What's welcome is your French disdain
    of dogma.
                 Quotations from Solon,
    Horace, Virgil and Plato,
    of course....
                 Digressions on food,
    ambition and fatherhood, assuredly....
But all in the spirit of conversation—
    without an angle, so to speak.
When you call marriage a "discreet
    and conscientious voluptuousness,"
    I partially agree.
                 After
    you explain that "valor" and "value"
    are etymologically akin, I see
    the connection.
                 Nothing seems
    contentious.
                 Your views on cruelty
    recall Tertullian's platitude
    that men fear torture more than death.
Of honors you are tolerant, noting
    that honors are most esteemed
    when rare and quoting Martial
    in support: "To him who thinks
    none bad, whoever can seem good?"
If mere consistency identifies
    small minds, you never were small.
One incident explains: perpetuating
    family names you called a vanity,
    and yet you willed your name

and fortune to your daughter's
youngest son.
                    Since she was married
twice and had two families,
two hundred years of litigation
followed.
                Why?
                        Because
Montaigne the grandpere silenced
Montaigne the philosopher, which proves
once more that irony, not reason,
rules the blood.
                    Otherwise,
your breadth of thought amazes me.
Each meal's a feast whose menu
    is the universe.
                        So here's a toast,
my friend, across four centuries.
To essays that seem to write
    themselves and sound like tabletalk.
To hospitality of mind where nothing
    is immune from scrutiny.
                        To all
that leaves me wisely confused
but even in confusion, wiser.

FACING THE LAKE WITH ST.-EX

A dozen mallards squawk
   in a shortarm vee above
   Lake Huron.
               Without a physicist
   among them, they slip each other's
   jetwash and wing northward
   equidistantly at cloud-speed.
I put aside the wartime prose
   of Antoine de St.-Exupery
   and track the ducks to Canada.
To be dull as a duck aground
   but awesome in flight and even
   more awesome in print describes
   St.-Ex in life and death.
If poetry is prose that soars,
   his prose in fact is poetry.
It made Consuelo overlook
   his dalliances, his sleight-of-hand
   with cards, his sudden absences.
How many men dare gravity
   with wings and words and win
   as no one did before
   or since or ever?
               Meanwhile,
   over the rhythm of waves
   the mallards are rowing the wind
   in perfect rhyme to show
   what's possible without instruction.

FOR ONE WHOSE NAME WAS WRIT ON WATER

Beds of impatiens flash
    their pinks and reds and whites
    like aging actresses pretending
    to look younger than they look.
Apple leaves begin their slow
    and spectral turning....
                       Two years
    before he hemorrhaged in Rome
    at twenty-six, John Keats
    dubbed fall a time "of mists
    and mellow fruitfulness."
                    I only see
    September and decay.
               Facing
    the worst of hells, poor Keats
    saw differently.
               To fall in love,
    then learn you're marked for death—-
    what could be worse than that?
But nothing in his poem says so.
Worse yet, the girl was immature.
While he lay starving "on a single
    anchovy a day, and a morsel
    of bread," she wrote him letter
    after letter he refused to read.
Autumnal as it sounds, I give
    the benefit of any doubt to Keats.
A red impatiens drooping
    from its sad stem's not sadder

than coughing lung-blood
on a linen pillow.
                    Keats
was a licensed surgeon.
                        He knew
the signs.
            If my September's
not the same as his, why quibble?
Spurning the worst, he conjured
    ripeness at its peak in one,
    two, three stanzas.
                    That speaks
a deeper poetry than doom.

BREAKDOWN

Like soldiers ordered to "Fall in,"
    platoons of starlings swoop
    and muster on a telephone line.
Equidistant and at birds' attention,
    they mimic ranks at "Parade rest."
Suddenly they dive into the air
    on cue, swirling in a bluster
    of wings like a dream gone mad.
For just that long, I think
    that madness rules the world,
    despite appearances.
                  "Change
    the rhythm," Pindar predicted,
    "and the walls of the city will fall."
It takes so little....
              Vary
    the height and width of any step
    by just a fraction, and the rhythm
    of a stairway dies.
             Change
    traffic patterns, and we slacken
    to the speed of doubt.
              Or let
come war, and we're undone
as if the sea breathed in
and never out against our shores,
surrounding, pounding, drowning
everything.
         It imitates what happens
when I'm writing, and the words
won't perch.

They swirl confused
as any flock in flight.
                    They're swirling
now.
        I'm losing touch
with what I should be saying,
and I can't remember what I think
I meant.
            The tempo's gone
completely....
                    Pindar was right.

ARMS AND THE WORD

Great sailors though they were,
    the Greeks abhorred the sea.
What was it but a gray
    monotony of waves, wetness
    in depth, an element by nature
    voyager-unfriendly and capricious?
Sailing in sight of shore,
    they always beached at night
    to sleep before the next day's
    rowing.
             Taming the sea
    by beating it with rods
    they named the ultimate insanity—
    a metaphor too obvious to paraphrase.
In short, they knew a widow-
    maker when they saw one.
                    Still,
    for honor, commerce or a kidnapped
    queen, they waged their lives
    against what Homer called wine-dark
    and deep.
             Some came back never.
Some learned too late that pacing
    a deck was far less hazardous
    than facing what awaited them
    at home....
             Homer would praise
    their iliads and odysseys in song.
Aeschylus, Euripides and Sophocles
    would watch and wait, then write
    of wars much closer to the heart.

They knew the lives of men—-
    no matter how adventurous—
    would end as comedies or tragedies.
They wrote that both were fundamentally
    and finally domestic.
                    Homer
    could sing his fill.
                  The dramatists
    dared otherwise.
                Compared
    to troubles in a family, they saw
    this business with the sea and swords—-
    regardless of the risk—as minor.

BUT YOU WERE WRONG

Not typically a thought, not
    anything conceived or earned
    but totally gratuitous....
                      It happened
    in your sleep, and, while it stayed,
    it made you memorize each minute.
Later, there was coffee to be drunk,
    your chin and cheeks to shave,
    slacks to be belted, shirts
    to be buttoned, ties to be knotted,
    and a world to awaken and name.
You watched a chief of state
    whose lone credential was audacity.
You listened every hour on the hour
    to the news.
              You read the telegrammic
    headlines and the columned texts
    that answered everything but why.
The more the present tense
    responded to the reveille of your complete
    attention, the more the echo
    of that perfect thought receded.
You said it would return
    with even greater emphasis,
    but you were wrong.
              Days
    intervened, then months, then years...
That thought was like the first girl
    you loved who loved you back.
Distance undid you both, proving
    that separation weakens a weak

love as surely as it strengthens
a strong one.
                    You felt
more bitter than bereft.
                              The world
remained the world where no one
stays twenty and desirable
for long.
                  But still a pressure
and an ache endured for half
a century as something undefinable
but unrepeatable that came
when you were least expecting it
and named its memory and left.

TO WAIT AS A WAY OF LIFE

Waiting to act is where
    the drama waits.
                    Act,
    and it's over.
                Bad gospel
for the overdoers of this world,
but irrefutable....
                    Hamlet pensive
is Hamlet at his truest.
                      A cobra,
coiled on its coils, is totally
cobra.
          The mountain snow
that keeps its avalanche a secret
threatens the deadliest with white
restraint.
             Never are brides
more beautiful than in their veils.
Sprinters at the starting blocks
    with all their muscles primed
    and flexed look equally supreme
before defeat or victory
undoes them.
              Look everywhere,
and everything's waiting to happen
next.
        Rifles are ready
in their racks.
          Lilacs are anxious
to become the first and only
versions of themselves.

                    Bombers
      are waiting with their waiting bombs.
Silently a cougar waits
      to charge a deer.
                    Its eyes
are hungry, but its claws are patient.

THE EYES HAVE IT

The eyes swallow whatever's
    there to see: a bluejay
    flirting with crumbs, telephone
    poles that stand forever
    at attention, bishops worn
    by their croziers and crowns, a not
    quite hidden naked couple
    joined at the loins below
    the Pont du Gard.
                The sheer
    perfection of sight prompted
    Hopkins to write: "...this sleek
    and seeing ball...but a prick
    will make no eye at all."
Misused, the same perfection
    haunted Donne: "But most
    the eye needs crossing, that can
    roam and move...."
                Quite true,
    but hardly all....
                Though hair will thin,
    and knees will ache, and privates
    contradict the orders of the brain,
    the eyes, even when failing,
    will demand to see—and see
    with clarity.
                They master us, and yet....
What sense but sight would anyone
    like least and last to lose?
How else does love speak out
    but through the eyes?

                    Bedouin
        mothers summon their children
        near by calling them "My eyes!"
And what are dreams but what
        the eyes remember while we sleep?
So, let them "roam and move"
        as they were born to do.
                            Our dreams
        need feeding, and the time is short.

LOOK UP, AND THEY'RE THERE

Planning to see them, I
   never do.
               Sometimes it's weeks
   or months without a glimpse
   although I spot the cloven
   echoes of their hoofmarks in the yard.
Once I glanced from the porch,
   and there they were—a doe
   and three "teenagers" browsing
   nose-down for bulbs.
               I let them
   browse, admiring their tawny
   pelts not yet gone winter-
   gray, the sleek sculpture
   of their skulls, the hard knots
   of not-yet-horns beside their ears.
After they sensed me near,
   the doe stepped grandly down
   the slope like a great actress
   after a curtain-call.
               The triplets
   stayed their ground, too inexperienced
   to know me as a threat or even
   as an interloper on their turf.
I raised my hand, and off
   they bolted in straight-up leaps
   but arched in flight like gazelles
   in panic.
               Tell me they carry
   Lyme Disease, and I'll agree.
Tell me how much they can destroy,

or how a hunter with his rifle
aimed might see no more
than venison on sixteen hooves,
and I'll agree.
                    But, God, the grace
of them, the poise, the way
they made me marvel at their wild
ease while they seemed totally
indifferent to their own perfection.

CONNECTICUT YANKEES

Each time my son was given
    gifts he had to keep
    but never craved, I'd try
    psychology and say, "Paul
    Moses would really like these."
His answer was, "Give them
    to Paul Moses."
             We never did
    but kept a closet full of unworn
    sweaters, puzzles still
    unpuzzled and games yet to be
    played....
          I think of this
    today while touring Mark
    Twain's house in Hartford.
From the porch I see what Twain
    had never seen: the East Hartford
    High School scoreboard, Children's
    Theater of Hartford and the Immanuel
    Congregational Church that posts,
    "What keeps faith fresh?" as this week's
    Sunday topic.
          Two souvenir
    shops—one for Twain, and one
    next door for Harriet Beecher Stowe—
    are hawking napkins, scented
    candles, T-shirts and coffee mugs
    that honor Mark and Harriet.
Frankly, scented candles put me off
    as much as asking what keeps
    faith fresh or what spawns faith
    in the first place?

At least,
that kind of faith....
                    "Always
do right," might have been Twain's
casual response, "This will
gratify some people, and astonish
the rest."
          Stowe's faith debunked
the myth of happy cotton-pickers
eating watermelon in idyllic
slavery.
          Asking if she can help,
the salesclerk points to Union
and Confederate caps beside the mugs,
candles and T-shirts.
                    I want
to say "Give them to Paul Moses"
but settle for "Just browsing."

FRIENDS, ROMANS, EVERYBODY

Who knows if ever it's enough
    to be reminded of how small we are?
Not how heavy or how tall
    but how miniscule in relation
    to the past, the distance from the earth
    to Mars, the fact that we're
    mere digits in the aging census
    of our kind.
            Nothing stifles
    braggadocio faster than that.
Had Hitler learned the skill
    of shrinkage as a boy, who
    would have ever seen him strutting
    in jackboots or sieg-heiling
    blackshirts in Berlin?
            He might
    have been content to be the house
    painter he started out to be.
In matters of belief, who knows
    why God, who needed no one,
    chose our littleness to be
    His own?
        For what?
            Your answer
    is as good as mine, and mine's
    a mouthful of silence.
            Since silence
    never lies, why bother with parades,
    the myth of dynasties, the soap-
    balloons of fame, or the fiction
    that bigger-and-better is best?

What else but diminution proves
　　a frank friend dearer than a fawning
　　fraud, defeated heroes braver
　　than victorious fools, and the heart's
　　wisdom stronger than the feast
　　of all excitements?
　　　　　　　　Seeing
how little can be much is all
that matters.
　　　　　　Even the small
point of my small pen in its small way
says nothing is bigger than that.

DEAR HEADSTONE

So far we're both the same
    years old—my name and I.
It plans to stay, which means
    it won't go with me when I go.
Shadows have the decency to fade
    when we no longer cast them.
Whoever's seen a posthumous
    shadow?
            But names last
    louder when we're gone.
                They come
    alive in contracts filed,
    paychecks cancelled, photos
    autographed or letters signed.
All that we are or were
    will be what someone might
    recall who hears them said
    or sees them printed in a book
    somewhere we've never been.
Sometimes my name and I
    don't speak.
            I say a name
    is only how I'm called,
    not who I am, so why
    the fuss?
            It tells me I'll be
    praised, dismissed or damned
    for what I'm called, and that's
    what names can do.
               How can I
    win this fight of two times
    one?

Although we're twins of sorts,
it promises to bury me.
                              It will,
of course, regardless and no
matter and despite.
                         Before
this argument began, it won.

FOR THOSE WHO ARE NOT THERE YET AND MAY NEVER BE

Whatever it is, they're still
   in search of it.
              The searching
   turns into their lives.
                 It's theirs
at breakfast, theirs in sleep,
theirs in their long days
as gobs or grunts, part-timers
at McDonald's, sophomores
with debts, or mates who married
much too young.
              They crave
the moon, and most go after it
like pushy starlets, boxers
on the make, appraisers on the take,
flatterers at corporate retreats,
or sellers of anything that sells.
Many become their own cartoons.
Not all....
        Somewhere a rebel
may surface or a random hero
or a saint or anyone who's man
or woman enough to suffer
public ridicule for private
reasons.
        Forget the well-to-do,
the silver-spooned inheritors,
the merely lucky or the privileged
who have the luxury to choose
their challenges.

These words are not
for them.
They're for possessors
of the belly-fire of the brave
who face the Hell's Kitchen
of their hopes where the real
hungers wait their chance.
They're for God's fools who struggle
in the midst of things while life
keeps happening, and everything's
at stake, and nothing is resolved,
and no one knows the outcomes in advance.

IN THE KEY OF PICASSO

Frankly, I admire more
    the way he looked at things
    than how he painted them,
    Guernica and his minotaurs excepted.
In the Madoura kiln he changed
    mere pottery to portraiture.
His dishes sported faces,
    and his pitchers sprouted ears.
That showed his ingenuity
    as did his dancing nymphs
    with hippopotamal thighs—-
    his bulls' heads fashioned
    from bike seats and handlebars—-
    his painting of the face of Gertrude
    Stein that came to be the face
    of Gertrude Stein.
                Like most of us
    he made an art from anything
    at hand the way a chef
    can make a soup from onions,
    escarole, tomato pulp and beef.
It helps us meet a need
    to re-create or name in our
    own words what's simply there.
Remarkable?
           Not really.
              Even
my grandson does it, and he's
only two.
         He picks old words
and smiles them new.

     "Today
is Friday, but sometimes it will be
Tuesday."
     That seems as effortless
and true as something by Picasso—-
and with the same glee.
     For me
it's more like servitude each time
I watch my mute pen hatching
words to tell me what I think
I see.
    I wait for interventions....
I'm waiting now to re-invent
 on paper something simple
as a smile or outrageous as a dish
with eyes.
     It might not happen,
or it might.
     There's no deadline.

IV

MOMENT OF TRUTH

The sculpted head of Gustave V
    scowls at a sundial park
    near the Place Massena.
                        Benches
    circle the dial.
             On one
    a woman in a walking cast
    rests her bandaged ankle
    on a package.
             On the next a man
    with a gray pigtail is arguing
    in angry German on a cellphone.
Cohesively chattering Japanese
    flock by.
          The last one
    in the flock's a boy outfitted
    in a New York Yankee
    uniform.
          He tries and tries
    again to coax a French
    pigeon closer with a crumb.
Strutting off like a Japanese
    general, the pigeon gargles
    and ululates in pigeonese.
From the last bench I watch
    this random comedy of characters
    ad-libbing in performance as they pass.
I'm here because I never
    drowned in Watertown, had orders
    to Lejeune and not Korea,
    was spared the last and lethal

stings of mudwasps on a rampage,
missed the jet that plummeted
in Hopewell.

        Common, unremarkable
reprieves have given me
this afternoon in Nice like someone
left unchosen from a lottery.
I watch.

    I realize how much
depends on chance.

        I recognize
the reckless amnesty of God.

CÉZANNE'S ATELIER NEAR AIX

It's as he left it, or as it
   left him after he painted it.
A sprawl of dappled quince,
    three pipes and two pairs
    of spectacles command a tabletop.
A crumpled tam relaxes
    at the opposite end.
                I think
    a lamp centers the two,
    but I could be wrong.
                Recently
    an ophthalmologist appraised
    the spectacles and saw how fuzzy
    and miscolored they made everything
appear.
           He wondered if Cézanne's
    whole alphabet of color
    erred as a result.
             Call it
    impressionism or call it
    a mistake, but Sainte-Victoire
    seems falsely brown beside
    the real thing.
           It's reminiscent
    of El Greco, isn't it?
             His portraiture
    of Christ and saints and bishops
    with their equine faces, upturned
    eyes and lengthened bodies
    wasn't Gothic, as the critics claim.

El Greco's optic flaw turned
    circles into ovals, ovals
    into candleflames, and horizontals
    somehow into verticals.
                    Like Paul
    Cézanne he painted what he saw
    though all he saw was wrong.
Astigmatism was his problem, not
    perspective.
               If what resulted
    was majestic, how do you explain it?
Does art transcend man's failings?
Do masterpieces simply happen?
Should art historians be qualified
    in ophthalmology?
                If you regard
    such questions as redundant
    or ridiculous, then you explain
    El Greco.
            You explain Cézanne.

THE LAST STOP BEFORE NOTHING

Dogs die braver than saints.
Women lying on their sides
 sleep softly hillier than men.
The huffs and puffs of lovers
 loving sound identical
 in every hemisphere.
 Such things
are obvious.
 Less obvious
is why each dog is like
no other—women sleeping
or awake are unrepeatably
themselves—all lovers have
specific names.
 What's clearer
seems closer.
 What's closer
grows dearer.
 Who cares if Samuel
 Johnson claimed that streaks in tulip
petals ranked as mere details
compared to generalities.
 I cherish
the details.
 They're the last stop
before nothing.
 They show us why
we're untranslatably ourselves
but still the living sum
of those who made us possible.

Our forbears sleep inside of us
    the way old English, older
    French, demotic Greek
    and Latin hide in plain
    American.
                    Who can deny it?
Ancestors from the Age of Stone
    and earlier, like mysteries
    we'll never master, come alive
    each time we breathe.
                    They say
    that we're the first and only
    of the last of many.
                    Smile,
    and our smiles are theirs.
Sing, and our songs have echoes.
There's no such thing as solitude.

LOOKING INTO A TULIP

"Have you ever looked into a flower, Mr. Gable?"
                                        Grace Kelly

Look in, and the flower stares back.
Its iris offers you the very
      whites, blues, pinks
      and lavenders of God.
                        Each petal
      revels in the final glory
      of itself.
                  For those distracted
      by horizons I propose five minutes
      in the company of tulips.
                              One
      tulip will suffice in all
      its purple understatement.
                        Look deep
      and see what's primping to its prime
      before it fades and falls,
      and you'll be mesmerized for life.
Brides in their wedding veils
      would understand.
                        They know
      it's not duration but expression
      that survives our days.
                        They flower
      in their one-time gowns
      just once for just one day.
Even though it ends, it stays.

GENE

No one would raise a presidential no
    against the headlines and the war....
Not the "new" Nixon stewing
    in New Jersey, still conniving,
    still the same.
                Not Hubert
Humphrey swilling cow's brains
near the Pedernales.
                    Not Bobby Kennedy.
Not even LBJ, the very President....
Almost unnoticed, you landed
    in New Hampshire, spoke
    to smallish but determined crowds
    and entered history.
               Who
    could have guessed your saga
    would include an abdication, murder
    in Los Angeles, a lost election
    and the Nixon follies?
              All
    for a war that bled on anyway....
Later there would be the mockeries:
    "Well born or not, he acts
    like a retired auxiliary bishop,
    a monsignor, St. Achilles
    sulking in his tent."
              Why bother
quoting them?
             Let them discover
    who you are in all your poetry
    and books.

As for the rest,
it's on the record...in the blood....
Heroes, of course, make everyone
uncomfortable.
They prod.
They won't

just go along.
They wake us up
when rather we would sleep.
If only seldom they prevail,
whoever claimed that heroism
guarantees salvation in advance?
In airports, dining rooms
and public places, people
understand and quietly salute you
with their eyes.
This proves
that heroes still define an epoch.
They are what we believe.
They last.

STILL, LIFE

Shakespeare, of course, was right.
Ripeness is all.
                Whatever's
ripely beautiful demands
to be stared at, memorized, copied.
That's why you paint.
                      Painting,
you forget you're born to die
by keeping what you see alive.
Last week you bunched a clump
of plums, just picked, beside
a sprawl of grapes, just picked.
For color you added eggplants,
black-purple as lake water
under the merest of moons.
Then—the green and reddening
cellos of pears, conical
apples, lemons from Sicily
the size of grapefruits flanked
by two bananas propped
in opposition like parentheses.
Later, the model—preferably
not a virgin, preferably still
in her twenties, preferably asleep.
Only a woman sleeping
or recently gratified presents
her body stripped of shame.
In short, a body totally
relaxed....
                Appreciating this
is not enough.

Possessing it
makes beauty just a dinner
for desire that's spent in the having.
Apples eaten are apples gone.
A woman *had* is suddenly
a woman lost.
But truly seen
and painted, she's a relish,
and the relish lasts and lasts.
See how you let the colors
speak.
The flesh of her inner
thighs matches the skin
of her throat.
Even asleep
her breasts seem partially awake.
You worked for days to paint
her pout as if it happened
from a breath just drawn.
And all
the time you worked, you never
thought, not once, of death.

BALLAD OF THE BROKEN TACKLE

If you're squat as a rock, and you know how to block,
and the backs that you block for are shifty,
you can dream of a life with a Hollywood wife
and a ranch you'll own outright at fifty.

But the jackpots of fame and your love of the game
never match what you learn as a player.
You crouch in the dirt, and you play when you're hurt,
and you wake up one day, and you're grayer.

Though nobody sees when you're gone in the knees
so you flinch when you're running or bending,
you feel in your heart that you're coming apart,
and you know when you're nearing the ending.

Jim Otto would glow with a big double-O
on the jerseys he wore in his glory.
Today he needs care, and he's wheeled in a chair,
and that's just one man and his story.

Look hard at the rest of the worst and the best
and notice how much they're reliant
on braces and canes and some pills for their pains
that have left them subdued but defiant.

The owners ate well while you sweated like hell
to give your home city a reason
to light up the sky like the Fourth of July
at the end of your winningest season.

Looking back you can see it's no bonus to be
number one in a league of achievers.
It just rouses the loud in the stadium crowd
and the rest of the paying believers.

Overlooking the noise, it's a game meant for boys.
At its best it's no more than a pastime.
But why were there tears despite all the cheers
when you limped off the field for the last time?

RAINS

Rainflakes spatter in ragtime
    on red shingles.
                Somehow
the rhythm suggests a fool
on stilts who's stilting nowhere,
stilt by stilt.
           Each
splatter's the size of a saucer.
By noon the rain's fog-faint
    as spray from the skrim of a wave.
By night it strengthens into sluices
    wallowing like wax on windshields
    and smearing even as it's wiped
    away.
         Shower, drizzle
or storm, it's all a matter
of seas sun-siphoned to the clouds
and then returned aslant or straight
as plummets to the bullseye world.
Rainfalls-to-be resemble rage
    or uncontrolled desire in the making:
    lowering clouds gone gray,
    thundrous kettle-drumming
    and the quick crack of dazzle
    down the sky.
                Leaves glisten
greener.
          Boulevards darken
with splashes.
            Square miles
of stippled open ocean
settle silently as loneliness.

But after the overture of buffalo
        thunder and the slashing flash
        of menace, there's such a steadiness.
In time the sprinkling down
        of cloud-high floodings fractioned
        into drops may float an ark
        or drown a new Atlantis.
                                Among
        quadrillions totally on target
        and aligned, they stay proportionate
        as poetry.
                        In all the languages
        of rain they say there's still
        a place for order, even
        in bluster, even in passion.

IT'S HOW IT ENDS THAT MATTERS MOST

Simply by being, they attract.
Berryman prayed to see them
    "as sisters or daughters."
                Simenon
    defined diversion as playing
    "with a new pair of breasts."
Blake the mystic thirsted
    "to find in wives what in whores
    is always found: the lineaments
    of gratified desire."
              And cummings
    wrote: "a pretty girl who naked is
    is worth a million statues."
Contrarily, most women see
    another woman naked as another
    woman only—same this,
    same that, same everything.
              Not so
    with many men who see them
    first as opportunities or prey
    or goddesses translatable in time
    to songs or poetry or art.
But hip-swish, lip-touch or any
    navel bared and staring
    like a brazen, single eye
    are only prefaces.
              The rest
defies anatomy.
              Edith
Piaf could arouse an audience
of men to adoration with a song,
one song.

Grace's smile kept
photographers at bay.
                    Ginger
became more beautiful the more
she danced.
            Each forte dazzled
like the fire in the center of a flower
or a gem.
            It flares again
each time a woman much desired
wears a name like Opal,
Dahlia, Ruby, Jasmine,
Beryl, Olive, Daisy,
Rose or, infrequently, Petunia.
Undressed or dressed, they linger
to be noticed as themselves, not
just another of the gender.
                        Is something
like desire at the root of this?
Probably—at worst one-sided,
but reciprocal at best.
                    Pleasure?
Some wonder who enjoyed it more—-
the leering elders as they watched
Susannah in her bath, or bare
Susannah knowing they were watching.

Love?
        Not instantly, of course,
    but over time a possibility
    since everybody needs it.
Luck or mystery?
                Who knows.
Seeing or hearing precedes it.

THE POEM THAT CAME AND WENT

The riptide surged, frothed
    and then surrendered in a garbled
    murmur to the shore.
                         It left
    asprinkle on the beach its random
    jewelry of shells and one
    mysterious tennis shoe.
Level as arrows barely inches
    from the waves, two seagulls
    skimmed in tandem while the clouds
    cast shadow-islands on the surface....
It was that kind of day,
    that kind of shore, that kind
    of weather.
                  Nothing forewarned me
    of a sudden, interrupting poem
    that would come intact, then flee.
Its echo dallied like a name
    or number I could never quite
    recall.
            Whatever it meant,
    it left me—after it left me
    forever—with a sense of ultimate
    perfection.
               In retrospect the words
    seemed certain and in place
    and quietly compatible.
                  What makes
    it now more sacred for the vanishing—
    the way a child lost

or not yet born is dearer
than all others or how a succubus
who disappears at dawn is even
more seductive in absentia?
It left an ache that prompts
the words I'm writing now.
Dante would understand.
                          How long
did he once look at Beatrice?
Six minutes?
                    Five?
                          He never
saw the girl again, and she
was just fourteen.
                          One glimpse
was all he ever needed
to renew his life, then turn it
into poetry that guided him like grace
and made a holy comedy of hell.

THERE'S MORE TO THIS THAN MOWING

"Imagine Sisyphus happy."
                    Albert Camus

You should respect the grain
        and action of the grass, align
        each swath so you allow
        some overlap and never scalp
        the roots.
                        You'll feel appeased
        to see the flowing lawn
        surrender to the blades that leave it
        like a crew cut in your wake.
Once by accident you over-ran
        a warren of wee rabbits,
        mangling one and scattering
        five more.
                        You stopped and worked
        your fingers down the funnel
        lined with rabbit fur to find
        the last survivor shaking
        like a sparrow in a sock.
                        Later
        you mowed across a nest
        of mud-wasps.
                        Twenty-seven
        stabbed you with their tails
        before you made it to the house,
        but still they kept on coming....
Normally you let your mind
        meander while you sweat
        the sweet sweat of hard work.

Even as you mow, you realize
this barbering is temporary
as yourself.
Each time you cut,
you feel already in arrears
but not to blame.
Is this
the same as shouldering a boulder
up a mountain, over and over?
Or is it just a green, sealevel
way of saying the relentless
must be tamed and reckoned with
repeatedly?
Or is it both,
and are they both the same?

LETTER TO BART

"Where is it we learn
Even things not worth doing
Are worth doing well?"
                    Barton Sutter

It starts with trivia: the crinkly
    tissue socks inside new socks,
    the bonus egg a boxtop
    recipe suggests for brownies,
    cuffbuttons on business suits
    that button nothing, neckties
    that tie no collar in its place.
Unnecessary, all of them.
Unnecessary too the varied shades
    of paint on cars, on walls,
    on surfaces in general.
                    Why bother
    with cherry, saffron, sandstone,
    puce, horizon, calico
    and flame when fundamental gray
    will cover?
                    Black or green,
    the hammer hammers.
                    Stew
    from a king's dish would taste
    no different ladled from a pot,
    and diamonds on a ring seem brazenly
    superfluous.
                    Had Shakespeare
    never lived, we'd get along
    quite well without his sonnets.

Compared to cash in hand,
    what can a sonnet buy?
And as for Homer?
                Why would
    a blind man rhapsodize a stupid
    war begotten by adultery
    and decided by a trick?
                    The fact
    that every war repeats the same
    stupidity is not the point.
The point is how whatever comes
    to be with no good reason
    we can see makes uselessness
    more precious than the usual.
A tissued sock is music
    to the fingertips.
                    An eggless brownie
    seems the poorer by one egg.
A colorless world might just
    as well not be.
                Why sonnets,
    weddings, dances, gardens,
    coins designed like jewelry?
Why jewelry?
                Why a backroad
    shrine of daisies in a jelly jar
    beside a doll of Christ
    that has no reason to be there
    at all?

And all in homage
to a God who chose, despite
divine alternatives, a totally
unnecessary way to die.

DEAD END

The road just stopped where woods
    began as if it somehow
    lost its purpose.
                Like lives
  too numerous to list, it died
  abruptly in full stride,
  headed for highways it would
  never reach.
           Straight as a bandage
  through the fields or looping
  like a lasso up a mountainside,
  its past was visible for miles.
It kept what all roads keep—
  a deep imperative of motion,
  beckoning the traveller in all of us
  to dream of destinations....
               What made
  the builders quit?
          Lack
  of cash or property disputes?
Or was it to remind inquisitors
  like me that there are finishes
  beyond anticipation?
             Lethal
  as lightning and as quick, they strike
  when they are least expected.
They contradict.
          They scrap our maps.
They say some destinations are
  the ones we're heading for, but some
  are not.
         Like roads that go
  so far but not a breath farther....

OURS

To paraphrase the Portuguese,
  God and marriages write straight
  with crooked lines.
      Our crooked
  lines reached forty-five today.
As usual it's just another day,
  but isn't every day just that?
We still share bread and bed,
  good news and bad, the never
  to be stated dread of who'll
  be left alone and when and how
  and where.
     That's up to God,
  of course, but still it rankles....
We know Camus was right
  to say, "All those who love
  and are apart know agony
  but not despair because
  they know that love exists."
What can I add that's truer
  than that?
     At thirty years
  I wrote that those whom the gods
  would destroy they first make happy,
  not distraught.
      You've made me happy
from the start.
     Without you I would
  surely be destroyed, but somehow
  we'd continue like a river or a road

that always seems to know
exactly where it's heading.
On this or any anniversary
that's certitude enough to make
our crooked lines run straight.

SEE-WORLD

You've seen the killer whales
    that will not kill, the sharks
    that will, the flouncing walrus
    and the clapping seals.
                What are
these manatees and Jacobites to you
but gullets waiting for a mackerel
when they do a trick?
             Until
you learn their names, that's all
they are.
         Each day your mother
and your father teach you names:
"moon" for the real moon, "baby"
for baby, "danger" for dangers.
It's Adam's legacy.
         We learn
to match an object with a name
and think we know the world
that way.
        But do we, really?
It's taken me my life to see
    that everything translates from what
    we say it is to what it's like.
Bridges are "shore linkers."
Jet engines are "furies in place."
Flowers are "reveilles in color."
A pruned oak resembles
    a hand with thumb and fingers
    amputated to the last knuckle....

Saying what you really see
        makes every minute a creation.
The world may claim you're
        nothing but a proper name
        or just the sum of everyone
        who's come ahead of you.
We know you're irreplaceably
        yourself, and that's much more
        because it means you'll be
        translated as you go like any
        work in progress.
                        Who cares
        if all the prophets in the world
        spell out your future in advance?
No one can give a name
        or time to possibilities before
        they're due.
                        Not even you.

TWO

Nothing pleads louder than a chair
    waiting to be sat in.
                    Nothing's
  as unfulfilled as tired suits
  aligned on hangers in a closet....
Outside my window sways
  an unswung swing.
                It lacks
 a swinger.
          Tulips pose like girls
  preparing for a long past prom.
Everywhere—absentia.
             Everywhere—
so many and so much in waiting.
I think of this while steadying
  my grandson on my lap.
                We've read
 his favorite book.
           We've said
 our rhymes.
          I've thought how right
 was Paz to say a face
 is never seen until it's loved.
I love my grandson's face.
His left cheek warms my right.
It's better than a kiss.
            How many
 predecessors shall we thank
 for changing now into this sacred
 second for the two of us?

It makes absentia an absence
   as if we've waited all our lives
   for what we hoped might happen,
   and suddenly it's ours, it's happening.

ONE DAY INTO THE WORLD

Clear, but with a chance of snow....
As forecasts go, that's usual
    since every day's born clear
    but subject to the chances.
                        You
    prove that true by suddenly
    arriving three days later
    than predicted.
                Watching you flex
your toes and fingers in your sleep,
we see that happiness is never
only being spared those losses
that would grieve us most but being
blessed by what we least expect.
Today we breathe abreast,
    and all the intervening decades
    fade like snow.
            Why ask for more?
Why are we here except to watch
    and wonder while we're here?
You answer that by being you—
    just you—on this first Wednesday
    of your just born year.

For Anna Catherine

JUST WORDS

In Arabic a single word
   describes the very act
   of taking a position.
                          Greeks
   pronounce three syllables
   to signify the sense of doom
   that all Greeks fear when things
   are going very well.
                      As for
   the shameful ease we feel
   when bad news happens
   to someone else, including
   friends?
                In Greek—one word.
To designate a hose that funnels
   liquid fire down the turret
   of a tank in battle, the Germans
   speak one word.
                  It's three
   lines long but still one word.
And as for John, Matthew,
   Mark and Luke?
                 There's not
   a surname in the lot.
                With just
   one name they match in memory
   the immortality of martyrs.
                 The longer
   they're dead, the more they live....
I praise whatever mates
   perception with precision!

                    It asks
us only to be spare and make
the most of least.
                    It simplifies
and lets each word sound final
as a car door being shut
but perfect as a telegram to God.